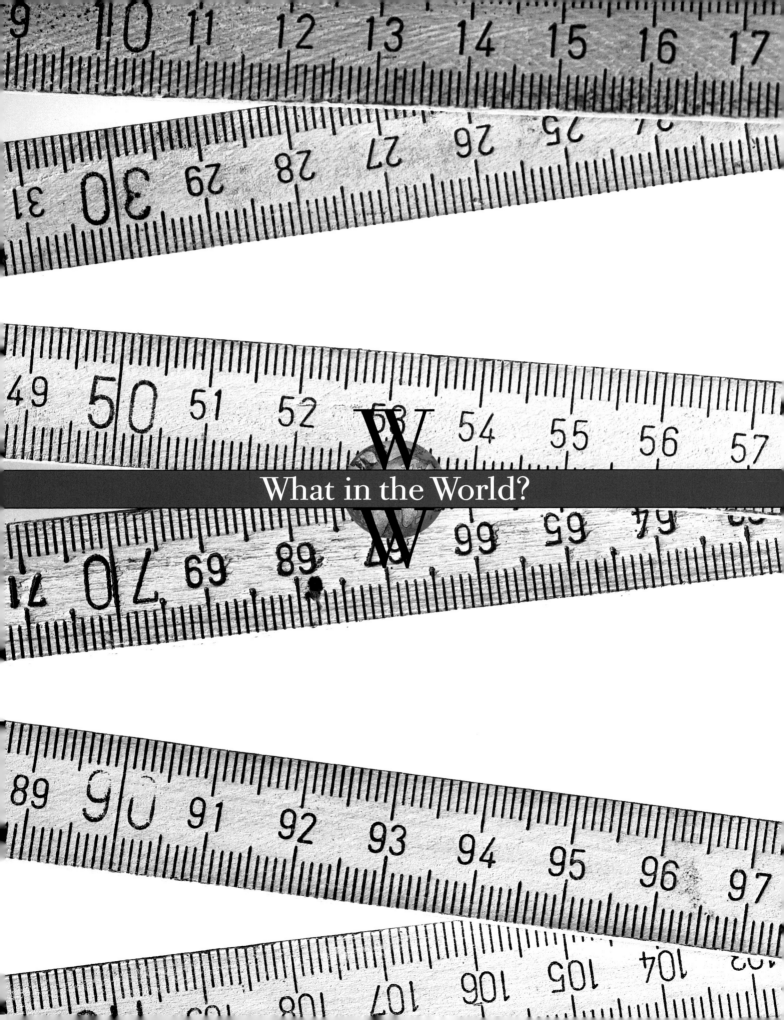

What in the World?

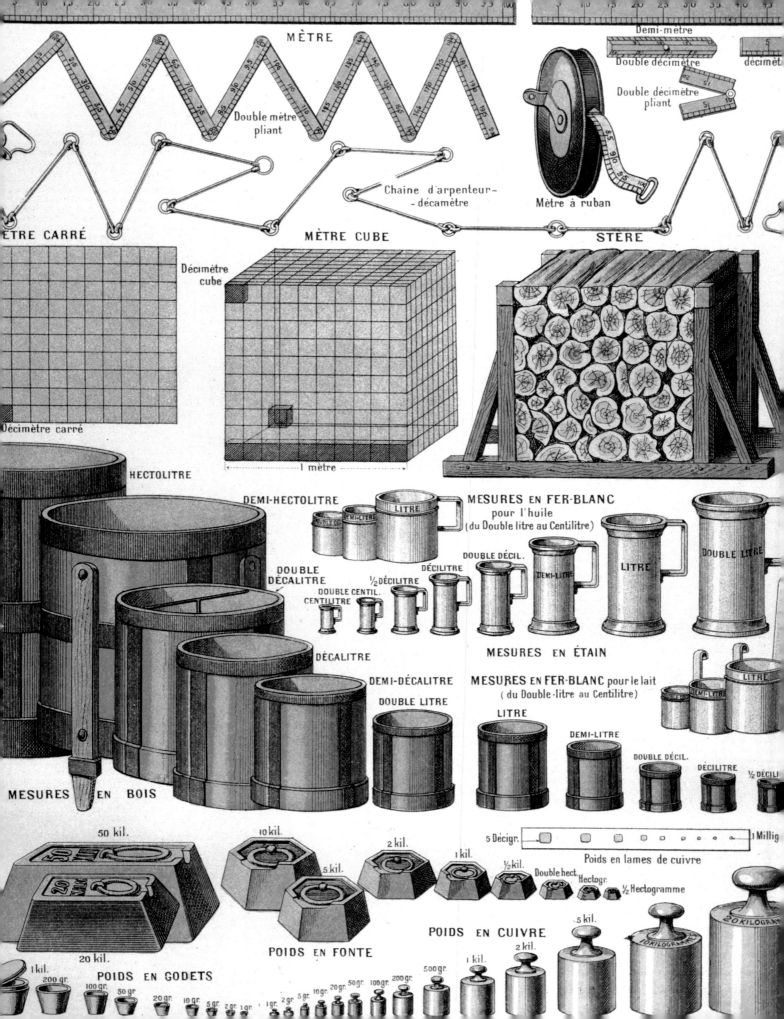

MÈTRE

Double mètre pliant

Demi-mètre

Double décimètre

décimèt...

Double décimètre pliant

Chaine d'arpenteur-
décamètre

Mètre à ruban

...TRE CARRÉ

MÈTRE CUBE

STERE

Décimètre cube

Décimètre carré

1 mètre

HECTOLITRE

DEMI-HECTOLITRE

DOUBLE DÉCALITRE

DÉCALITRE

DEMI-DÉCALITRE

DOUBLE LITRE

DOUBLE DÉC...

DEMI-LITRE

LITRE

DOUBLE CENTIL.
CENTILITRE

½ DÉCILITRE

DÉCILITRE

DOUBLE DÉCIL.

DÉCILITRE

DEMI-LITRE

LITRE

MESURES EN FER-BLANC
pour l'huile
(du Double litre au Centilitre)

DOUBLE LITRE

LITRE

DEMI-LITRE

MESURES EN ÉTAIN

MESURES EN FER-BLANC pour le lait
(du Double-litre au Centilitre)

LITRE

DEMI-LITRE

DOUBLE DÉCIL.

DÉCILITRE

½ DÉCIL...

MESURES EN BOIS

50 kil.

20 kil.

10 kil.

5 kil.

2 kil.

1 kil.

½ kil.

5 Décigr.

1 Millig...

Poids en lames de cuivre

Double hect.
Hectogr.
½ Hectogramme

POIDS EN FONTE

POIDS EN CUIVRE

5 kil.

2 kil.

1 kil.

500 gr.

1 kil.
200 gr.

100 gr.

50 gr.

20 gr.

10 gr.

5 gr.

2 gr.

1 gr.

1 gr.
2 gr.
5 gr.
10 gr.
20 gr.
50 gr.
100 gr.
200 gr.

500 gr.

10 KILOGRAMMES

20 KILOGRA...

POIDS EN GODETS

The Metric System

Jennifer Fandel

Creative Education

Introduction

In 1792, at the north and south ends of France, suspicious townspeople surrounded two quiet French astronomers. The men, Jean-Baptiste Delambre and Pierre Méchain, had been seen climbing mountains and bell towers, surveying the area and making notes. The people eyed their strange, shiny instruments and in angry tones demanded explanation. Were they spies? What business did they have there? In the heat of the French Revolution, as French citizens were overthrowing the government and rulers were struggling for power, the scientists were working toward something just as revolutionary. In the journals they carried lay the foundations of the metric system, a new way of measuring—and seeing—the world.

The Greek philosopher Eratosthenes is considered the father of geodesy, or mathematics relating to the shape and size of Earth. His measurements taken in the third century B.C. came within 10 percent of today's known measurements.

People have long used equipment such as telescopes and surveying instruments (above) to examine Earth and the skies.

The French Revolution of 1789–99 was widely championed by the country's large population of peasants.

Reason and Revolution

The quest for a universal system of measurement began in 1789, at the start of the French Revolution, when the world was being transformed by radical new ways of thinking. In the minds of many European scholars of the time, intellectual progress was being hampered by traditions, religion, and emotions. Pushing these aside, the scholars turned to logic and science to better understand the world. This faith in reason was the heart of the Enlightenment Movement, which spread across Europe throughout the 1700s. Enlightenment scholars believed that knowledge, like a flame, would illuminate the path of humankind, making unending progress and achievement in fields of science and thought possible.

Denis Diderot, a French philosopher and writer, published the world's first encyclopedia from 1751 to 1772. In 17 volumes, the encyclopedia covered everything from farming to philosophy and included pictures of activities such as ironworking and weaving.

The French title page of Denis Diderot's Encyclopedia, or a Systematic Dictionary of the Sciences, Arts, and Crafts.

The cotton gin, which was usually operated by slaves, brought about a dramatic increase in U.S. cotton production.

In the United States, Enlightenment ideas were tested in the country's quest for freedom from British rule. During the American Revolution (1775-83), Americans fought for the right to govern themselves. But the writers of 1776's Declaration of Independence saw the possibility for much more. Believing that individual freedom was a natural and rational idea, they wrote that all people were created equal and were guaranteed "life, liberty, and the pursuit of happiness" under the new government. Paradoxically, many Americans accepted the extreme inequality that brought African slaves across the Atlantic Ocean.

In 1792, American inventor Eli Whitney created the cotton gin to remove the sticky seeds from cotton. Instead of one pound (.45 kg) of cotton, a single person could now clean 50 pounds (23 kg) of cotton a day.

The U.S. Declaration of Independence, penned by Thomas Jefferson, was officially adopted on July 4, 1776.

In CONGRESS, July 4, 1776.

The unanimous Declaration of the thirteen united States of America

When in the Course of human events, it becomes necessary for one people to dissolve the political bands which have connected them with another, and to assume among the powers of the earth, the separate and equal station to which the Laws of Nature and of Nature's God entitle them, a decent respect to the opinions of mankind requires that they should declare the causes which impel them to the separation. — We hold these truths to be self-evident, that all men are created equal, that they are endowed by their Creator with certain unalienable Rights, that among these are Life, Liberty and the pursuit of Happiness. — That to secure these rights, Governments are instituted among Men, deriving their just powers from the consent of the governed, — That whenever any Form of Government becomes destructive of these ends, it is the Right of the People to alter or to abolish it, and to institute new Government, laying its foundation on such principles and organizing its powers in such form, as to them shall seem most likely to effect their Safety and Happiness. Prudence, indeed, will dictate that Governments long established should not be changed for light and transient causes; and accordingly all experience hath shewn, that mankind are more disposed to suffer, while evils are sufferable, than to right themselves by abolishing the forms to which they are accustomed. But when a long train of abuses and usurpations, pursuing invariably the same Object evinces a design to reduce them under absolute Despotism, it is their right, it is their duty, to throw off such Government, and to provide new Guards for their future security. — Such has been the patient sufferance of these Colonies; and such is now the necessity which constrains them to alter their former Systems of Government. The history of the present King of Great Britain is a history of repeated injuries and usurpations, all having in direct object the establishment of an absolute Tyranny over these States. To prove this, let Facts be submitted to a candid world.

He has refused his Assent to Laws, the most wholesome and necessary for the public good. — He has forbidden his Governors to pass Laws of immediate and pressing importance, unless suspended in their operation till his Assent should be obtained; and when so suspended, he has utterly neglected to attend to them. — He has refused to pass other Laws for the accommodation of large districts of people, unless those people would relinquish the right of Representation in the Legislature, a right inestimable to them and formidable to tyrants only. — He has called together legislative bodies at places unusual, uncomfortable, and distant from the depository of their public Records, for the sole purpose of fatiguing them into compliance with his measures. — He has dissolved Representative Houses repeatedly, for opposing with manly firmness his invasions on the rights of the people. — He has refused for a long time, after such dissolutions, to cause others to be elected; whereby the Legislative powers, incapable of Annihilation, have returned to the People at large for their exercise; the State remaining in the mean time exposed to all the dangers of invasion from without, and convulsions within. — He has endeavoured to prevent the population of these States; for that purpose obstructing the Laws for Naturalization of Foreigners; refusing to pass others to encourage their migrations hither, and raising the conditions of new Appropriations of Lands. — He has obstructed the Administration of Justice, by refusing his Assent to Laws for establishing Judiciary powers. — He has made Judges dependent on his Will alone, for the tenure of their offices, and the amount and payment of their salaries. — He has erected a multitude of New Offices, and sent hither swarms of Officers to harrass our people, and eat out their substance. — He has kept among us, in times of peace, Standing Armies without the Consent of our legislatures. — He has affected to render the Military independent of and superior to the Civil power. — He has combined with others to subject us to a jurisdiction foreign to our constitution, and unacknowledged by our laws; giving his Assent to their Acts of pretended Legislation: — For Quartering large bodies of armed troops among us: — For protecting them, by a mock Trial, from punishment for any Murders which they should commit on the Inhabitants of these States: — For cutting off our Trade with all parts of the world: — For imposing Taxes on us without our Consent: — For depriving us in many cases, of the benefits of Trial by jury: — For transporting us beyond Seas to be tried for pretended offences — For abolishing the free System of English Laws in a neighbouring Province, establishing therein an Arbitrary government, and enlarging its Boundaries so as to render it at once an example and fit instrument for introducing the same absolute rule into these Colonies: — For taking away our Charters, abolishing our most valuable Laws, and altering fundamentally the Forms of our Governments: — For suspending our own Legislatures, and declaring themselves invested with power to legislate for us in all cases whatsoever. — He has abdicated Government here, by declaring us out of his Protection and waging War against us. — He has plundered our seas, ravaged our Coasts, burnt our towns, and destroyed the lives of our people. — He is at this time transporting large Armies of foreign Mercenaries to compleat the works of death, desolation and tyranny, already begun with circumstances of Cruelty & perfidy scarcely paralleled in the most barbarous ages, and totally unworthy the Head of a civilized nation. — He has constrained our fellow Citizens taken Captive on the high Seas to bear Arms against their Country, to become the executioners of their friends and Brethren, or to fall themselves by their Hands. — He has excited domestic insurrections amongst us, and has endeavoured to bring on the inhabitants of our frontiers, the merciless Indian Savages, whose known rule of warfare, is an undistinguished destruction of all ages, sexes and conditions. In every stage of these Oppressions We have Petitioned for Redress in the most humble terms: Our repeated Petitions have been answered only by repeated injury. A Prince, whose character is thus marked by every act which may define a Tyrant, is unfit to be the ruler of a free people. Nor have We been wanting in attentions to our British brethren. We have warned them from time to time of attempts by their legislature to extend an unwarrantable jurisdiction over us. We have reminded them of the circumstances of our emigration and settlement here. We have appealed to their native justice and magnanimity, and we have conjured them by the ties of our common kindred to disavow these usurpations, which, would inevitably interrupt our connections and correspondence. They too have been deaf to the voice of justice and of consanguinity. We must, therefore, acquiesce in the necessity, which denounces our Separation, and hold them, as we hold the rest of mankind, Enemies in War, in Peace Friends. —

We, therefore, the Representatives of the united States of America, in General Congress, Assembled, appealing to the Supreme Judge of the world for the rectitude of our intentions, do, in the Name, and by Authority of the good People of these Colonies, solemnly publish and declare, That these United Colonies are, and of Right ought to be Free and Independent States; that they are Absolved from all Allegiance to the British Crown, and that all political connection between them and the State of Great Britain, is and ought to be totally dissolved; and that as Free and Independent States, they have full Power to levy War, conclude Peace, contract Alliances, establish Commerce, and to do all other Acts and Things which Independent States may of right do. — And for the support of this Declaration, with a firm reliance on the Protection of divine Providence, we mutually pledge to each other our Lives, our Fortunes and our sacred Honor.

John Hancock

Button Gwinnett
Lyman Hall
Geo Walton.

Wm Hooper
Joseph Hewes,
John Penn

Edward Rutledge.

Thos Heyward Junr.
Thomas Lynch Junr.
Arthur Middleton

Samuel Chase
Wm Paca
Thos Stone
Charles Carroll of Carrollton

George Wythe
Richard Henry Lee
Th Jefferson
Benja Harrison
Thos Nelson jr.

Robt Morris
Benjamin Rush
Benja Franklin
John Morton
Geo Clymer
Jas Smith
Geo Taylor
James Wilson
Geo Ross
Caesar Rodney
Geo Read
Tho M:Kean

Wm Floyd
Phil. Livingston
Frans Lewis
Lewis Morris

Richd Stockton
Jno Witherspoon
Fras Hopkinson
John Hart
Abra Clark

Josiah Bartlett
Wm Whipple
Saml Adams
John Adams
Robt Treat Paine
Elbridge Gerry
Step Hopkins
William Ellery
Roger Sherman
Sam el Huntington
Wm Williams
Oliver Wolcott

W.J. STONE SC. WASHN.

Although 98 attackers and only 1 defender died in the storming of the Bastille, the attackers ultimately captured the prison.

Inspired by the fight for freedom in the U.S., a group of French citizens attacked the Bastille, the jail and royal arsenal in Paris, touching off the French Revolution in 1789. For decades, farmers, laborers, and shopkeepers had grown increasingly discontent as the French monarchy took much of their earnings in high taxes. While King Louis XVI lived in splendor in his royal palace of Versailles just outside Paris, peasants starved, unable to afford the high price of bread. The king was executed in 1793, and over the next 20 years, the country remained in political chaos.

Louis XVI, king of France from 1774 to 1792, in his ornate royal robes.

The gate of a former slave fort in the African nation of Benin, once a center of the slave trade.

Southward from there, the gradual banning of the slave trade in European countries brought widespread effects to the continent of Africa. In Sierra Leone, a country in western Africa, Britain established an independent colony for freed slaves who wished to return to their native land. With the education and skills obtained during their lives as slaves, some of Sierra Leone's new residents became Christian missionaries and set up trading businesses with other African nations.

In 1791, on the Caribbean island of Hispaniola, native people began their fight for freedom from French rule. The natives would eventually gain their freedom in 1804.

By the time the slave trade came to an end, millions of Africans had been taken forcibly from their homeland.

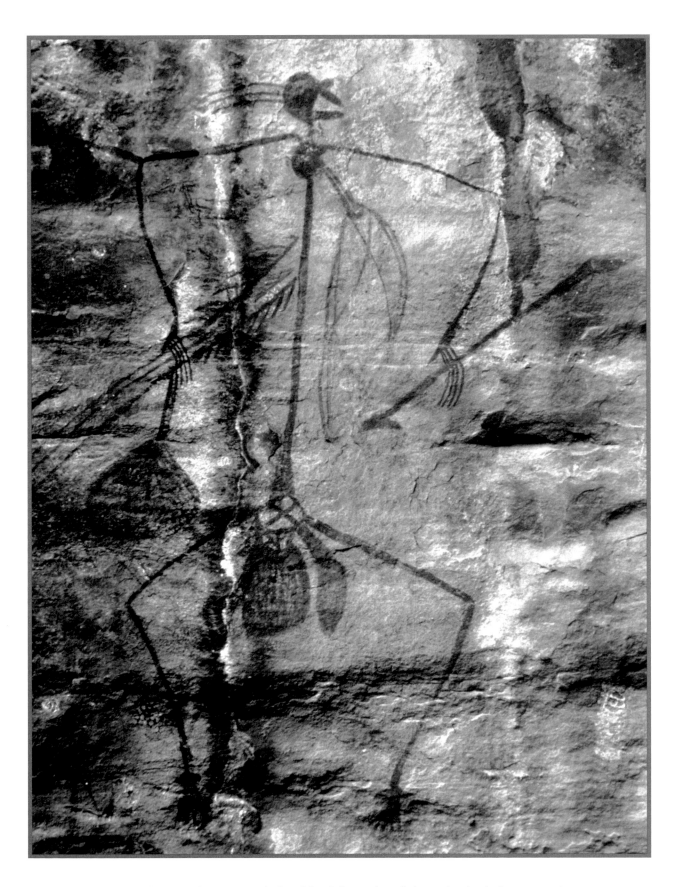

Australia's Aborigines created many cave paintings (above); lemons (opposite) were found to both prevent and cure scurvy.

In 1794, the British navy tested the first prevention treatments for scurvy, a debilitating disorder caused by a lack of vitamin C. After sailors consumed mandatory rations of lemons, only one fell ill with the disorder.

Australia's Aborigines, first encountered by outside peoples in the late 1700s, are considered the world's oldest culture. Over thousands of years, they developed specialized tools, such as boomerangs and spear throwers, to help them hunt wombats, bandicoots, and kangaroos.

Farther east, across the Indian Ocean, the British established a penal colony in Australia in 1788. Their arrival put them in contact with a culture relatively unknown at the time: the Aborigines. A seminomadic people, the Aborigines lived in temporary, cone-shaped homes made of piled branches. To survive in Australia's deserts, they had learned to bake bread from the ground seeds of desert grasses, and to discern which insects were palatable. As the new British arrivals struggled to grow food and tend livestock on Australia's hot, parched lands, the native Aborigines continued to thrive.

Hokusai Katsushika's The Wave *exemplifies the Japanese art of woodcut printmaking developed in the late 18th century.*

North of Australia, developments in agriculture caused China's population and economy to expand at a rapid pace. Faster-growing rice, better irrigation techniques, and new crop rotation practices gave the country a reliable food source and helped different regions specialize in different goods for trade. Textiles came from central China, while porcelain was produced in the southeastern part of the country. By the end of the 18th century, the country's population had swelled to 300 million people, more than in all of the countries of Europe combined.

Porcelain was first developed in China, where vases and other wares were decorated with striking images.

In 1796, Catherine the Great, Russia's queen, died after 34 years on the throne. Although despised by some for her authoritarian rule, she expanded Russian power and established Russia's first diplomatic ties with Europe.

English physician Edward Jenner pioneered the first smallpox vaccine in 1796. Two years later, he invented inoculation, the practice of injecting a virus into a person to fight disease. His discoveries led to longer life spans.

Russia's Queen Catherine the Great saw herself as an Enlightenment thinker.

Against this backdrop of revolution and growth, a group of French scientists looked beyond the chaos erupting in their country and imagined a way to link the corners of the world. As the 1700s neared an end, and as scientific developments and increased knowledge about other cultures improved lives around the world, France's Enlightenment scientists sought a means of improving international trade and communication. These men strove to put the measure of the world in people's hands.

An Enlightened Path

The seven Enlightenment scientists who created the metric system were born in France between 1733 and 1752. During the 18th century, France was the center of Europe's Enlightenment Movement, with its government providing financial support to scientists of the highest merit, many of whom belonged to the prestigious Academy of Sciences.

The men of France's Academy of Sciences were motivated by an unquenchable desire for knowledge about the world. Among them were chemists such as Antoine Lavoisier, who uncovered the composition of water and other substances. There were mathematicians such as Marie-Jean Condorcet, who worked on theories of probability, and Adrien Legendre, a statistician who perfected calculations for measuring Earth's surface. Also among the Academy's members were physicists such as Pierre-Simon Laplace and Jean-Charles Borda. Laplace developed and tested theories concerning Earth's shape, while Borda invented the repeating circle, an instrument for measuring and mapping the planet.

The French writer and critic Voltaire was considered one of the leading voices of the Enlightenment. Known for his comic phrasing, intelligence, and biting wit, Voltaire was occasionally jailed and was exiled to England for several years.

A portrait of Voltaire (opposite); Antoine Lavoisier conducting a chemical experiment in his laboratory (above).

Most of the products needed by citizens of 18th-century France were purchased at local markets.

In 1791, Marie Fontaine Havel, a French farmer's wife, created Camembert cheese. She packed it in lightweight wooden boxes for shipment around the world, spreading its popularity. The soft cheese is still packed in wooden boxes.

In the late 1700s, the people of France used more than 250,000 different units of weights and measures, and these units went by nearly 800 different names. For years, this had appalled the Academy's scientists. They realized that as long as people of different regions used different measurement systems, efficient trade and communication would remain difficult.

In their frequent discussions, the Academy's scientists reasoned that a uniform measurement system, if developed correctly, would facilitate the exchange of goods and information throughout France. For a while, however, these big ideas never left the meeting room. While they believed in the logic of their ideas, the scientists were long daunted by a major obstacle: people's natural reluctance to abandon old ways.

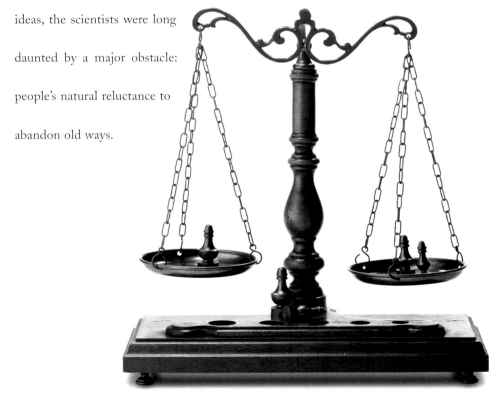

Balance scales were once commonly used for weighing commodities such as spices, tea, and thread.

In 1790, after France's nobility and clergy were pushed out of power, the country's new government, known as the National Assembly, wanted to make a clean break from the past. No longer satisfied with systems of measurement based on tradition or the rule of royalty, the government promised the people of France "one law, one weight, and one measure." Prompted by the new government's aspirations, five willing Academy members—Marie-Jean Condorcet, Antoine Lavoisier, Pierre-Simon Laplace, Jean-Charles Borda, and Adrien Legendre—immediately formed the Commission of Weights and Measures. Recognizing that the government's decree was the force they needed to finally implement a national measurement system, the scientists put aside their own work to dedicate themselves to the task.

But why not go one step further and create a worldwide measurement system, the scientists wondered. They believed that people far beyond France's borders would likely come to accept a uniform system too if it were based on something common to all peoples and cultures, such as the measurement of Earth. Because most people perceived Earth as both universal and eternal, the scientists hoped that people would come to see their measurement system as universal and eternal as well.

In 1793, Paris' Louvre art museum opened to the public. The building, previously one of the French king's palaces, exhibited many works of art confiscated from nobles and aristocrats from the old French regime.

In 1789, France's National Assembly wrote the Declaration of the Rights of Man and Citizen, which set forth the rights of all men: liberty, property, security, and resistance from oppression.

For 200 years, beginning in the early 1600s, artists lived and worked on the lower floors of the palace that became the Louvre.

Among the Louvre museum's many treasures is the bejeweled crown worn by King Louis XV at his coronation.

A FAUT ESPERER Q'EU JEU LA FINIRA BEN TOT.

l'éduleur en Campagne Ap. 1789.

A political cartoon of the French Revolution, depicting the nobles and the clergy riding on the back of the peasants.

To help spread the revolutionary message, citizens of France formed their own political clubs in the 1780s and 1790s and handed out revolutionary newspapers and pamphlets in the streets. Cafes were the favored places to discuss politics.

One of the French scientists' early ideas was to base the new measurement system on the length of a pendulum as it swung in one second. This was considered troublesome, however, because it based one unit (length) on another (time).

To simplify their mission to measure Earth, the scientists decided to use one portion of the planet as representative of the whole. They already had in their possession a 1740 measurement of the French meridian, an imaginary line running from Dunkirk, a city at the northern tip of France, to Barcelona, a city off France's southern edge in northern Spain. Yet the scientists wrestled with the fear of error. If this measurement system was to be eternal, the scientists wanted absolute perfection. To achieve this, they asked two of their best astronomers, Pierre Méchain and Jean-Baptiste Delambre, to physically measure the French meridian for themselves.

Mapmaking was well-established by the time the Commission of Weights and Measures decided to measure the French meridian.

Méchain and Delambre, both born in the 1740s, came from modest families and reached their positions by spending every bit of free time on their passion for the stars and planets. Méchain, working as a government mapmaker by day, devoted his nights to astronomy and discovered 11 comets. Delambre worked as a tutor and studied astronomy on his own, although his interest wasn't kindled until he was in his 30s. While Méchain's discoveries earned him entrance into the Academy of Sciences in 1782, Delambre wasn't voted into the Academy until February 1792. Yet only three months after joining the Academy, Delambre was chosen by his distinguished peers to measure the meridian in the northern part of France.

Eighteenth-century astronomers studied earlier charts of the sky, such as this chart depicting one theory of planetary orbits.

Once the standard measurement for the meter was established in 1799, a meter bar was forged out of platinum to make the measure official.

The records of Pierre Méchain and Jean-Baptiste Delambre are currently housed in the Observatory of Paris. Filling 20 cartons, the records include all of their computations, maps, diagrams, and formulas.

Jean-Baptiste Delambre (1749–1822)

Pierre Méchain (1744–1804)

An illustration of the port city of Dunkirk, France, in the 18th century.

In 1802, German explorer Alexander von Humboldt and his French partner Aimé Bonpland climbed a volcanic peak in the Andes Mountains of Peru. The peak, measured at 19,700 feet (6,005 m), was the highest altitude climbed and measured at that time.

On maps, the distance between Dunkirk and Barcelona seemed easy enough to traverse in only a year. What maps could not illustrate, however, were the obstacles Méchain and Delambre would face: changing battlefronts during the French Revolution, difficult weather, and a varied, often rugged, terrain. A distance measured by a simple hand's breadth on a map would become hundreds of miles and seven years on land beneath the two scientists' feet.

While measurements of the French meridian were beginning, to the southeast, in Italy, Mount Etna (opposite) was erupting.

A Measure of the World

Beginning in the summer of 1792, standing at the northern and southern ends of France, respectively, Jean-Baptiste Delambre and Pierre Méchain focused their eyes on surveying instruments. Taking careful measurements of the landscape along the French meridian, they recorded the data in journals. The scientists soon ran into problems, however, that would add an unexpected six years to the project.

Along their journey, both men were detained—by suspicious towns-people, government officials, and the French military—and questioned about their work.

While Delambre's carriage traveled on many difficult roads, Méchain had to travel by horse or mule through some of France and Spain's most wicked terrain. Additionally, Méchain encountered snow on the summits of the Pyrenees Mountains and heavy rains in the valleys, weather that made traveling, let alone measuring, nearly impossible.

Before the metric system's creation, some areas of France measured land in footsteps. In other areas, farm fields were measured in *homme* and *journée*, indicating how many men and days were required to work the land.

A view of some of the gentler terrain of southern France, where vineyards dot the countryside.

By the time Delambre and Méchain measured the French meridian, equipment more advanced than the compass had been invented.

Many consider Death of Marat *to be the finest work by Jacques-Louis David, the foremost painter of the French Revolution.*

French painter Jacques-Louis David, a leading figure in the revolution, was known for his politically inspired paintings. *Death of Marat,* **finished in 1793, portrays the stabbing of a leader who is relaxing in a bath.**

In 1792, France implemented the guillotine, a machine used for beheading, as a method of humane execution. More than 17,000 people were executed using the guillotine during the Reign of Terror, a particularly brutal period during the French Revolution.

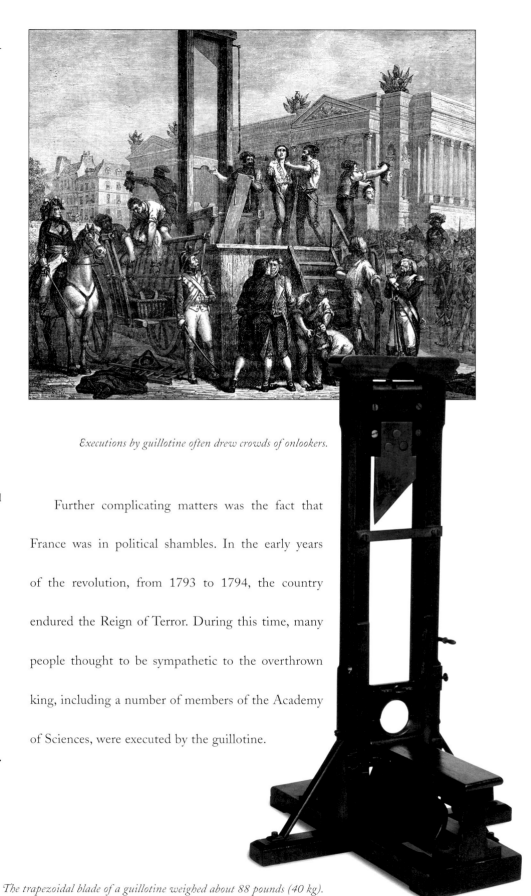

Executions by guillotine often drew crowds of onlookers.

Further complicating matters was the fact that France was in political shambles. In the early years of the revolution, from 1793 to 1794, the country endured the Reign of Terror. During this time, many people thought to be sympathetic to the overthrown king, including a number of members of the Academy of Sciences, were executed by the guillotine.

The trapezoidal blade of a guillotine weighed about 88 pounds (40 kg).

As Méchain and Delambre carried out their measurements, the Commission of Weights and Measures in Paris decided to set the base unit of the new measurement system close to an *aune*, a distance of about three feet (.9 m). The *aune*, common to much of France, was a unit used for measuring cloth. The scientists hoped that using a familiar base measurement would make it easier for people to accept and learn the new system.

Using prior calculations of Earth's surface, the scientists determined that one 10-millionth of the distance from the North Pole to the equator would bring them close to an *aune*. So, using Méchain and Delambre's measurements of the French meridian, the scientists would first calculate the distance from the equator to the North Pole, including adjustments for irregularities in Earth's shape, then divide that distance by 10 million to find the base unit of length.

Before the French Revolution, most men in France wore breeches or pantaloons, and women wore wide dresses.

Revolutionary playing cards portrayed trousers (opposite), writer Jean-Jacques Rousseau (above left), and "Justice" (above right).

Both ancient Greek columns (opposite) and modern domes (above) rely on accurate measurements.

Since the beginning of the modern Olympic Games in 1896, the metric system has been used to measure Olympic races. The 1896 Olympic marathon was 40 kilometers (24.9 miles) long, slightly shorter than today's 42.2-kilometer (26.2 miles) race.

Meanwhile, the new French government settled on a name for the in-progress base measurement. It would be known as the meter, from the Greek word for "measure." The measurement system would be called the metric system, meaning "the system of the meter." In 1793, the scientists discussed using the Greek and Latin prefixes *milli*, *centi*, *deca*, and *kilo* to make small and large measurements easier to read and understand.

While the French were developing the metric system, in Japan, art depicting ordinary people and scenes flourished.

In the spring of 1799, seven years after starting their measurement work, Méchain and Delambre presented their completed data to French and international scientists. Unfortunately, the scientists uncovered a major problem. The data suggested that Earth was more uneven than the scientists had previously believed. In other words, the meridian through France really *didn't* represent the rest of Earth.

While this was a great scientific discovery, it made calculating the official length of the meter more difficult. As they worked out the distance from the North Pole to the equator, the international scientists voted to use old adjustment figures instead of the new information to reconcile Earth's irregularities (while they didn't know it at the time, this decision would actually make the meter measurement less accurate as a reflection of Earth's size). They then divided this number by 10 million to arrive at the meter's length, equal to 39.37 inches.

Part of the metric system's appeal is that its units of measure are based on multiples of 10.

After the meter was made official, the scientists formally established metric weight measurements. The measurement for the metric gram, the base measurement for weight, relies on a length measurement, so it couldn't be officially determined until the meter was known. In 1799, scientists defined the gram as the weight—in precise temperature conditions—of one cubic centimeter of rainwater. While the official meter unit was important for measuring such quantities as land and cloth, the scientists knew that the weight measurement would have a greater immediate impact, especially when it came to measurements of food in town markets.

Since the development of the metric system, people around the world have weighed produce and other goods in terms of grams.

The metric system, once fixed in place by the scientists' data, fell under the control of the erratic French government. In 1801, Napoleon Bonaparte, France's head of state and soon-to-be emperor, made the metric system compulsory, declaring, "Conquests will come and go, but this work will endure." Ten years later, however, Napoleon turned France back to its old measures. He knew that the French people were not using the metric system, and he himself complained that the system was too difficult to learn. In a change of heart, Napoleon mocked the scientists, stating, "It was not enough for them to make 40 million people [France] happy, they wanted to sign up the whole universe."

Between 1793 and 1804, Napoleon Bonaparte rose from a military general to the emperor of France. While successful in his reforms of French law, Napoleon was ruthless in his quest for power and an expanded French empire.

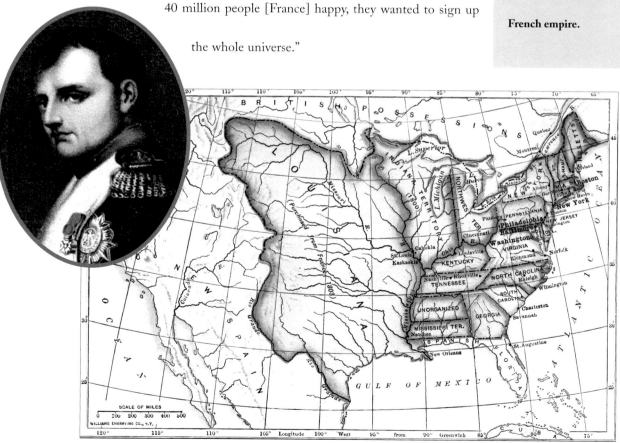

France once held the vast American territory of Louisiana, but in 1803, Napoleon Bonaparte sold it to the U.S.

The newly adopted metric system soon became part of the everyday life of French merchants, traders, and craftsmen.

Today, road signs around the world give the distance between destinations in kilometers (1 kilometer is 1,000 meters).

But sign up the universe they did. In 1840, as France expanded its trade and empire into Africa and Asia, it again declared the metric system mandatory and put the Greek and Latin prefixes into use. By that time, many nations around the world had seen the advantages of using a uniform measurement system for communication and trade. Now, more than 200 years after Méchain and Delambre's painstaking survey of France's landscape, nearly every country of the world has signed on. As the Academy of Science's Marie-Jean Condorcet once stated, the metric system has become a measurement "for all people, for all time."

Due to advances in science, the meter was redefined in 1983 as the "distance traveled by light in a vacuum in 1/299,792,458 seconds." Every redefinition of the meter throughout history has preserved the meter length established in 1799.

SYSTÈME MÉTRIQUE — MESURES DE SURFACE
UNITÉ : **le Mètre carré.**

The metric system was developed for the benefit of scientists, traders, mathematicians, and inventors alike.

The late 1700s and early 1800s were marked not only by scientific advances, but also by new diversions, such as the circus.

1789	The French Revolution starts, and France's Academy of Sciences begins discussing a national measurement system.
1791	France's new government accepts the Commission of Weights and Measures' plan for an Earth-based measurement system.
1792	Pierre Méchain and Jean-Baptiste Delambre begin their measurement of the meridian through France.
1794	English poet, artist, and visionary William Blake publishes his *Songs of Experience.*
1795	Spanish painter Francisco Goya finishes his famous painting *The Duchess of Alba.*
1799	Delambre and Méchain present their data to the first international conference of scientists.
1801	The first asteroid, Ceres, is discovered by Giuseppe Piazzi, an Italian astronomer.
1803	The world's first food cannery opens in France to supply food to emperor Napoleon Bonaparte's armies.
1813	Throughout Europe, people listen and dance to the newly popular waltz.
1815	Thousands in the East Indies die when the volcano Tamboro erupts on Sumbawa Island.
1818	British writer Mary Shelly's famous tale of horror, *Frankenstein,* is published.
1819	Spain's art museum El Prado, designed to house Spanish painting and sculpture, is completed after 34 years of construction.
1821	France's exiled emperor, Napoleon Bonaparte, dies.
1823	The Macintosh raincoat is invented when a Scottish inventor bonds rubber to cloth.
1831	British naturalist Charles Darwin documents plant and animal life in South America and the Galapagos Islands.
1834	French educator Louis Braille pioneers a new reading method for the blind, calling it Braille.
1835	American P.T. Barnum, a showman and circus developer, begins his career by exhibiting the "world's oldest living woman."
1840	The metric system is finally made the official measurement system of France.

Copyright

Published by Creative Education
123 South Broad Street, Mankato, Minnesota 56001

Creative Education is an imprint of The Creative Company.
Design by Rita Marshall, Production design by Melinda Belter

Photographs by Alamy (Black Star, Classic Image, Danita Delimont, Garry Gay, Hemera Technologies, Bill Howe, ImageState, Lebrecht Music and Arts Photo Library, llianski, Mary Evans Picture Library, Nikreates, North Wind Picture Archives, Per Karlsson – BKWine.com, Pixoi Ltd, POPPERFOTO, Visions of America, LLC, Visual Arts Library (London), Richard Wadey, Henry Westheim), The Bridgeman Art Library (The Bastille Prison, 14th July 1789 (oil on canvas), Dubois, Jean (1789–1849) / Musee de La Ville de Paris, Musee Carnavalet, Paris, France, Giraudon. T801 Map of Africa, from the "Theatrum Orbis Terrarum," pub. by Ortel Ortelius (1527–98), Antwerp, c. 1570, NO_DATA / © Royal Geographical Society, London, UK), Art Resource, NY (Giraudon, Erich Lessing, The Pierpont Morgan Library, Réunion des Musées Nationaux, Scala), Getty Images (Andreas Cellarius, Takuya Inokuma, Barry Rosenthal, RYOICHI UTSUMI), The Granger Collection, New York (page 28, page 43), museé d'art et

d'archéologie de Laon (France) et Photo J.P. Jorrand
Illustrations copyright © 2006 Tom Curry (5), © 2007 Etienne Delessert (cover, 1, 3, 11, 46, 48), © 1993 Editions du Seuil (37, 39)

Library of Congress Cataloging-in-Publication Data
Fandel, Jennifer.
The metric system / by Jennifer Fandel.
p. cm. — (What in the world?)
Includes index.
ISBN: 978-1-58341-430-9
1. Metric system—Juvenile literature. I. Title. II. Series.

QC92.5.F36 2006   530.8'12—dc22   2005050690

First Edition
9 8 7 6 5 4 3 2 1

Index